Painting Flou on Silk

Lydie Ottelart

Search Press

Contents

Finding the inspiration

'Say it with flowers' is the theme of this book and I have planned it with all those who say they cannot draw in mind. Your aim should be to achieve your own original designs to whatever standard you desire, but I suggest that you begin by following my demonstrations.

Practice the following:–

1) Select any flower and then reproduce this faithfully by transferring each detail on to squared graph paper. First place each petal on the paper and trace round the contours. Then make a separate tracing of each part, such as the stamen, pistil, calyx and sepal, first detaching these from the original sample.

2) Having analysed each part in this way, now rearrange the flower again, in order to study it once more as a whole:–

a) Viewed from above. A dot can indicate the centre from which the petals radiate, making sure that they are correctly spaced.

b) Viewed from the side. This should indicate the stalk and calyx. Draw the corona and sepals, then the middle petal followed by those adjoining it.

c) Viewed at an angle. Draw an ellipse and very lightly mark in the heart of the flower about half-way up, then place the petals round it.

d) Viewed as a bud. At an early stage of growth, a bud will be seen as a single petal overlapping the rest. Later on, two or three petals will open.

3) Whatever format you intend to use, such as a square, rectangle, circle in a square or oval in a rectangle, first draw several horizontal and vertical lines with a ruler on to your background, or concentric circles with a compass, in order to achieve a balanced effect. In the space defined by these preliminary guidelines now outline complete flower shapes, seen at various angles and remembering to include some buds.

4) You must now consider the question of stylisation. This means the simplification of the natural form but without loss of the flower's individuality. Constant sketching will provide a wealth of graphic ideas on which original work may be based. As a beginning, try copying some of the sketches shown here.

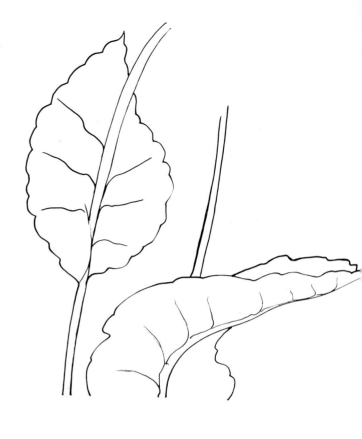

Selecting the flowers

Five different flowers have been chosen for detailed study. These include full-face, side view, at an angle, bud formation, leaves and stalks. Please note that the characteristics belonging to each of these groups are selected for features in common, rather than for botanical accuracy.

1) Very simple types, such as the daisy and sunflower. Also the buttercup, primrose and fruit blossoms, such as apple, cherry, pear and plum.

2) Flowers which have their petals arranged round a visible centre, such as the poppy, anemone and the water-lily.

3) Flowers with trumpet-shaped corollas, such as the convolvulus, campanula and the arum lily.

4) Complex flowers with dense petal formation. These include the rose, peony, dahlia and chrysanthemum.

5) Long-petalled flowers, including the iris, lily, tulip and orchid.

These are just some examples of the many thousands of different types found in nature. To begin a detailed and minute study of a specific flower you will probably need to make from four to six sketches of each section, before your design is ready to paint on silk.

Five or six designs from each of the above categories and all based on detailed studies will be explained and illustrated in this book. A wide range of materials and techniques has been used to encourage you to experiment. Given an imaginative approach, every variation contributes its own individual effect.

Equipment and materials

Make it your aim to choose a different material for each new technique studied. Your studio, or working area, should be light and well-aired, with running water and an electric plug available. Your work-table should be to a comfortable height, say 90cm (36in).

Frames

During painting, the silk is usually wet and has to be fully suspended without touching any surface. To stretch the silk on a wooden frame use drawing pins or, preferably, three-pronged pins and push them into the frame at intervals of about 4–5cm (1½–2in).

The frame should consist of four lengths of wood about 2 × 2cm (¾ × ¾in) thick, mitred at the corners and joined, or four lengths of wood slotted at the corners and glued together. You can also obtain a metal frame but this is very heavy and it requires special fixings for the silk.

Before the silk is stretched on to a wooden frame, cover the frame with adhesive tape. It can then be wiped clean and remains of paint from a previous work will not spoil a new piece of silk.

Brushes

Use a brush to apply paints to silk. This should be of good quality but not necessarily made of hair. One fine brush and a thicker one will usually be sufficient for your needs.

To cover large surfaces with the same colour, rather than a brush use a piece of cotton wool soaked in the required colour. Special foam brushes can also be obtained for this purpose.

Silk paints

Readily-available liquid silk paints have mostly been used for the projects given in this book. These may be diluted with water or 95° proof ethyl rubbing alcohol, a mixture of both, or with a special dilutant. In some techniques, artist's watercolour paints, or specially thickened pigments, may be used.

When using traditional silk painting methods, the completed painting must be 'fixed' as recommended by the manufacturer to ensure that the colours do not fade with exposure to the light, or disappear in laundering, but even with expert fixing, painted silk does lose some of its radiance after the first wash.

There are three methods of fixing but you *must* follow the instructions given by the manufacturer and never mix different brands of paints and fixatives.

Iron-setting paints are the most popular. These are fixed by ironing at the temperature recommended by the manufacturer, and are referred to as 'thermofixable'.

Brush-on fixative in liquid form. This is brushed on after the paints are dry and left for the recommended period of time, then removed by washing.

Steam-setting paints are usually alcohol-based, but traditional colours may be used. They are fixed by steaming in a purpose-built electric steamer, but, as an alternative, it is possible to use a pressure cooker.

Fabrics

Silk is the perfect background for a painting but certain types of wool, or cotton fabrics may also be used.

Silk

This can be purchased in many different textures, ranging in width from 90 to 140cm (36 to 56in) and in weight from 80 to 140 mommies. The mommie system of weight gauge was devised by the Chinese and is universally used in the wholesale silk trade to determine the thickness of the silk.

The different types of silk fall into the following categories:–

1) Pongé. A fine-grain silk. The higher the classification number the heavier the silk.

2) Crêpe. There are many different varieties and weights, including crêpe de Chine, Moroccan crêpe and crêpe georgette.

3) Muslin. A soft, gossamer-fine fabric.

4) Textured silk. These have a raised surface, such as the ribbed effect of twill and are difficult to paint.

5) Shiny silk. These have a smooth surface, such as satin.

6) Figured silk. These feature self-coloured patterns, such as brocade.

Pure silk can be identified by unravelling the warp and weft threads from a piece of fabric, rolling them together and setting light to the extreme edge. Having burnt for a few millimetres (¼in), the silk forms a charred ball and the flame goes out. A smell of burning horn also occurs.

When the cocoons are unusable as thread because of breaks in the weaving, they form what is called 'floss silk'. When two silk-worms combine to form the same cocoon, they produce mingled threads of a thick and irregular weave, used for textures such as dupion. Wild silk, or tussah, is produced by wild or semi-domesticated worms.

To launder silk, wash by hand. Wash separately in lukewarm water with a gentle soap product – do not steam, soak or wring. Rinse well and roll up immediately in a soft, colour-fast terry towel. When still damp, iron at a low temperature.

Techniques

There are many ways of applying paint to fabric and each one produces a different effect. Simplest of all is to paint directly on to wet silk and let the colours flow into each other but you have no control over this technique. The following methods explain how to separate one colour from another.

Wool
Open-weave wool is not really suitable for painting but very fine worsted wool, wool crêpe and also mixtures of silk and wool may be used.

Wool fabric comes in a variety of widths, suitable for shawls, but it is best to experiment on a small remnant to see what effects you can achieve. Wool also requires a longer fixing time.

Cotton
Fine, closely-woven cotton and mixtures of cotton and some man-made fibres are suitable for painting. Always wash the fabric first to remove any dressing, which will prevent the paints from penetrating the fibres.

Enlarging or reducing motifs
Throughout this book diagrams are given of flower motifs which you can copy but to enable them to fit into the page size, many of them have been reduced. To enlarge the motif, or reduce it still further, you can use a photocopier, or purchase a pantograph from an art or craft shop. This device consists of four flattened rods and at the appropriate points, a tracing point and a drawing point is fixed to the rods. The pantograph is hinged at the crossing points and can be adjusted to enlarge or reduce the copy.

Wax method
This silk painting technique has been borrowed from the craft of batik. This age-old art evolved around the principle that wax and liquid repel each other, so certain areas of the fabric are treated with hot wax before the dye is added, thus blocking out this colour. In silk painting, very subtle effects can be achieved by using blendable pigments, rather than dyes, and this method is known as 'false batik'.

Types of wax
Paraffin-wax is the most popular choice and is sold in blocks. It is white and can be obtained from chemist shops. It adheres well to the surface but has a tendency to crack. Beeswax also comes in blocks and is a browny-beige colour. Used on its own it gives virtually no cracking at all. Other types of wax are also available but it is a question of experimenting to see which one suits you best.

A mixture of 30% beeswax and 70% paraffin-wax is referred to as 'Javanese' wax and this flows very smoothly. A mixture of 40% beeswax and 60% paraffin-wax will produce a firmer consistency, suitable for drawing. A wax prepared especially for batik is available from craft shops.

Using wax
1) Use pure paraffin-wax for a dividing line between colours.

2) Use a mixture of two-thirds paraffin-wax to one-third beeswax to block out an area when overlaying two colours.

3) Use a mixture of half paraffin-wax to half beeswax to block out areas when overlaying several colours.

4) A mixture of two-thirds beeswax to one-third paraffin-wax is suitable for covering large areas.

5) Pure beeswax is very rarely used but is suitable when cracking is to be avoided.

Preparing wax
A wax pot is used specifically in batik for melting and heating the wax to give the right consistency and this is the most efficient method. The design of this pot is such that you do not run the risk of spilling hot wax. They are available from most craft suppliers.

If you do not want to go to this expense, wax can be heated in a double saucepan, kept for this purpose.

When the mixture contains more paraffin than beeswax, you could also use a feeding-bottle heater or depilatory-wax heater. Paraffin-wax melts at a lower temperature than beeswax, but both give off smoke when over-heated and lose their permeability.

Brushes for wax
Choose those with long, hard bristles. You will need a thick, wide brush to cover large areas, a round, pointed brush or a flat, narrow one for precise outlines and a fan-shaped brush for special effects.

A special tool used in batik, called a 'tjanting', is recommended for drawing fine lines and details. It has a small metal receptacle to hold the warm wax, with a shaped spout for pouring and is held by a wooden handle. Tjantings are light to handle and easy to use and are available from craft shops.

Applying wax
The use of wax has two essential functions: 1) it separates two colours and, 2) it protects one or several colours already applied. Each process is explained when used in the examples featured in this book.

Paraffin-wax is the most popular choice but all types and mixtures must flow freely and adhere to the fabric and this depends solely on achieving the correct temperature. Mistakes made at this stage are not easy to rectify, so test that the wax is ready for use on a scrap of the silk. When it appears transparent it has penetrated the cloth but if the wax appears opaque, it is not quite hot enough.

Before fixing the silk, the wax must be removed without damaging or wetting the silk. The best method is to flake off as much wax as possible, then place the silk between layers of absorbent paper and on several sheets of newspaper. Iron, using the correct temperature setting for the fabric, constantly changing the paper as it becomes saturated with wax.

Consistency of gutta
Gutta may thicken in a warm temperature, as well as in handling, so be sure to check its density before use. The thicker the silk being used, the more fluid the gutta, and vice versa. Very thin gutta will spread and allow the colours to intermingle and very thick gutta is difficult to spread smoothly and will not dry easily.

The gutta can be diluted with a few drops of a special solvent which is available for this purpose. To test the gutta, dip a toothpick into the liquid and hold it over a mixing cup; if it forms a thin trickle the consistency is right.

Coloured gutta
Gold and silver gutta can be obtained from craft shops but it is a simple matter to colour it by adding one or two droplets of typographic ink or silk paint. Test the colour on a scrap of silk first and either add more paint for a brighter colour, or a few drops of solvent for a more subdued shade.

Applying gutta
With this technique it is vital to keep each colour separate from the next with a firm, unbroken line of gutta, to achieve a stained-glass effect. Whether using an applicator, or a paper cone, it should be held like a pencil but do not slant it too much. Before beginning, lightly press the tip to expel any air or to remove dried gutta.

Form the outlines of the design slowly, avoiding any creasing of the silk by your arm movement. An even pressure and speed is needed to control each line from start to finish and each one must be unbroken. Where the gutta has been applied the paint is prevented from penetrating the fabric and areas of different colours can be kept separate.

Gutta-percha method
This is undoubtedly the most popular technique used in silk painting but it requires patience and practice to reach a high standard. Gutta-percha is a rubber substance, light-beige in colour, with the consistency of thin honey and is usually referred to as 'gutta'. This is used to draw the outlines of a design and to separate the colours from each other.

The best way to apply gutta is with a metal-tipped applicator bottle but a suitable alternative is a cone made from tracing paper. To make a cone, cut a rectangle 14 × 18cm (5½ × 7in) from the paper. Fold the paper at an angle of 30 degrees towards the top edge, then roll the paper round the triangle to form a cone. Make sure that the hole at the point is not larger than a fine needle or pin. Roll a small piece of adhesive tape round the point, taking care not to cover the hole, then close the remaining openings with tape, leaving the top into which the gutta will be poured open.

It is important to check the completed gutta outlines of a design against the light before beginning to paint. In that way, any breaks, or lines which are too thin, can be seen and corrected.

Gutta lines applied to white silk will remain white after the painting has been fixed and washed. Where coloured, or gold and silver gutta has been used, these colours will show as lines. When the painting has been fixed the gutta can be washed out, or removed with dry-cleaning liquid. Gold and silver gutta should *not* be dry-cleaned.

Anti-fusant method

Paints applied side-by-side on wet silk will run into each other like watercolours. If you want to work without wax or gutta, but still don't want the colours to mingle, the silk can be impregnated while it is still dry. With this method you can restrict the fluidity of the paints and employ many of the techniques used when working on paper or canvas.

Preparing anti-fusant

A ready-made medium is available from craft shops but this is intended for silk of a medium weight and may not be suitable for the silk you have chosen. Also, some products are diluted with water and if you intend to apply a background to the silk first, this will be ruined.

To make your own anti-fusant, use one part gutta to from four-to-seven equal amounts of solvent but bear in mind the degree of viscosity needed for the silk. There are no hard-and-fast rules and you must experiment with a scrap of silk to find the correct amounts, but as a guide fine silk will require a ratio of one-to-four, while very heavy silk will need one-to-seven.

This mixture will keep well when properly bottled and stored away from light and heat.

Applying anti-fusant

This medium does not affect the painting whether it is used on top of the paint or underneath it. It is therefore possible to apply a background colour to the silk first, preferably light in tone, then allow this to dry thoroughly. This is a useful hint, as it is difficult to apply a completely smooth background over an impregnated surface.

Using a piece of cotton wool soaked in the anti-fusant mixture, cover the silk working in parallel bands across the surface. Do this very thoroughly, even if your design is not intended to cover the whole area, otherwise gaps will show in the completed painting. Allow to dry slowly.

You can now paint directly on to the dry silk without the risk of any colours merging. Work quickly so that liquidity can be maintained and your washes kept smooth and even. Let each colour dry, noting that a hair-dryer can be used to speed this up, before placing the next one beside, or over it. The paints will not penetrate the silk and will only show on the side actually painted.

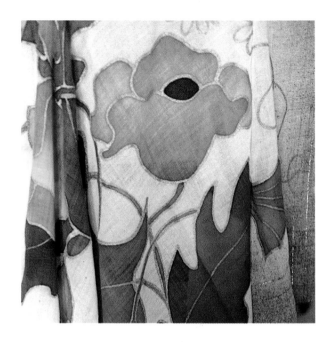

This method is not really suitable for articles of clothing or household linen, as it causes the silk to lose its suppleness. One other slight disadvantage is that the silk sometimes 'yellows' after fixing.

Template method

This method allows you to repeat a similar motif indefinitely, using a wide range of colours on many different types of fabric. The templates are cut from cardboard, or firm transparent plastic, with a choice of different sized pointed blades. Bristol-board is easy to cut but tends to curl and will only last for a limited period. Laminated paper is equally easy to cut, lasts longer and does not absorb colours, so it can be wiped clean with a damp cloth after use. Transparent plastic templates make reproduction more accurate.

Designing templates

Transfer your choice of drawing to the board, then follow the drawn contours with a blade, pressing hard enough to perforate the board cleanly. (It helps to place a sheet of glass under the board.) The motif you have cut out, the *positive*, and the space it will leave, the *negative*, may both be utilized.

If the design is complicated, first draw it directly on to the board, then simplify the shapes, visualizing the spaces between as well as the actual outlines. The golden rule to observe is that all the empty bits must be joined by 'bridges' of board to avoid your template falling apart! Shade in the parts which are to be cut out, making sure that the bridges are as narrow as possible.

If your design is to be in more than one colour you will need a template for each one. First carry out the above processes to prepare your initial drawing. Now divide the motif into the number of colours you intend to use and transfer each component of the template to a separate board. Exact proportions must, of course, be maintained and each board, or template, confined to one of your colours. When all are superimposed, the effect should reproduce your original design.

Now cut out your templates, using different sized blades to cut cleanly into corners and difficult areas. In order to reproduce lines and bands, use adhesive tape. For lettering, buy suitable stencils or metal templates.

Applying to the fabric

You can apply the motif to all types of material, such as silk, fine wool, cotton, linen, nylon, polyester and rayon, but always wash the fabric first. The surface can be smooth, rough, velvety or spongy but it is best to select one which does not have a highly-embossed pattern. Washing the fabric first in warm water, or soaking in a solution of warm water and soda crystals should reduce any surface 'nap'.

It is *important* to make sure that the paints you use have a creamy consistency which will cover the surface easily and completely. Apply the paint to the dry fabric with a brush which has short, hard bristles. For your work-area you will need a large, isolated table. Cover with a soft, thick towel, with a sheet of absorbent paper, such as blotting paper, placed on top.

Spread out your fabric until it is completely flat and unwrinkled, ironing it first if necessary. If you are decorating a pillow-slip or tee-shirt, place a sheet of absorbent paper between the front and back layers. Mark the position where you intend to place the template with thread or pins. Place the template in position and secure it with adhesive tape. If you use the positive template you will achieve an outline but the best results are obtained with the negative template.

Preparing the paint

To prepare your colours use a palette of china, or plywood, and mix with a palette-knife. Do not dilute. Before beginning to paint check that colours, even from the same range, are compatible and can be fixed by ironing to make them washable, light-resistant and permanent. The consistency of the pigments may vary according to each manufacturer but additives for thickening paint to produce a raised surface are available.

Dip your brush into the paint but do not over-fill it, in case surplus paint finds its way under the edges of the template. Tap the brush over a sheet of paper to remove any excess. Always wash your brushes after use and remove any stains instantly with soap and water.

Applying the paint

Holding your brush vertical, carefully guide it round the outer edges of a *positive* template, or the inner contours of the *negative* template. If you wish, the colour for a negative can be graduated in tone and depth of colour, or you can use a stippling or blot technique to achieve interesting effects.

Gently remove the template and rinse and dry it before use on a different area. Allow the paint to dry thoroughly, particularly if you are using several colours for each motif.

When you have completed the painting the fabric must be ironed, adjusting the temperature to suit the type of material. The design itself must also be carefully ironed and it helps to place a sheet of plain paper between the iron and the fabric for this purpose. The painting can now be washed just like any printed material and this will also help to remove any initial hardening.

Sugar-syrup method

This amazing technique produces sensational results, causing out-of-focus blends of colour, or a marbling effect. The syrup is used in the same way as wax to block out certain areas of colour, around which you can then paint. The painting must be left to dry for a considerable time, certainly not less than 24 hours, and during this process the wet paint and the syrup react with each other so that the final design evolves in an unpredictable way.

Preparing sugar-syrup

Mix an equal volume of powdered sugar and water – a large wineglass of each will be sufficient for a small area. Bring the mixture slowly to the boil, watching the surface as the syrup gradually thickens until the bubbles grow larger and burst more slowly. This is the exact moment to remove the mixture from the heat, to avoid browning.

The syrup will thicken as it cools. It can be used tepid or cold and can be kept for several days in a glass receptacle. Should it crystallize, dilute it with a little boiling water and then repeat the heating process.

Applying the syrup

If you wish to apply an overall background colour, do this first on wet silk and leave this to dry thoroughly.

As the sugar-syrup dissolves when wet, you must now work on *dry* silk, applying the syrup liberally. All types of brushes, as well as sponges of any size and shape can be used to apply the syrup to the dry background, but try using corks and bottle stoppers for interesting effects. You can apply the syrup in stripes of varying length and thickness, or just as blots in specific areas, but you must work rapidly and not allow the syrup to dry before beginning to paint.

Now apply the paints to the areas between the syrup. These should be applied broadly, using a soft brush and without worrying about painting over the outlines of the bands of syrup. If you wish you can repeat this whole process, allowing the silk to dry and adding further areas of syrup stripes then finally adding more colour. Leave to dry thoroughly before fixing the paints. This may take several days according to the room temperature and the degree of dampness in the atmosphere.

Fix the paints by steaming in a purpose-built steamer at a moderate temperature, protecting the fabric on both sides by a double thickness of absorbent paper. During fixing the sugar-syrup melts and leaves a paper-thin residue on the silk which must be removed by washing.

Watercolour method

This is an art rather than mere craftsmanship, as the flow of paints is not controlled by an agent, such as gutta. It is possible, however, to limit the way in which the paints merge into each other and this is a fascinating task. The freedom acquired by mastery of this technique will be worth all your practice and efforts!

Materials

A suitable frame; tacks; silk; ordinary watercolour paints; two or three watercolour brushes of good quality but not too fine; a mixture of water and 95° proof alcohol and a plentiful supply of clean water.

Preparing the silk

Do not use impregnated silk. Place the silk in the frame and dampen it all over, but do not saturate it or it will shine.

Keep a jar of water on hand for dampening the silk if it begins to dry out, another jar for cleaning brushes, plus a small jar of the water-alcohol mixture. Keep a piece of rag handy for wiping your brushes and some kitchen paper to dry the wet silk.

Painting the silk

Your colour range should be limited, of medium intensity, as well as some pure tints with black added for tone variation.

Sketch in your design employing light, clear colours. Your brush-strokes must always follow the shape of the forms you are depicting and should echo the basic 'rhythms' of the subject. Use middle tones and finish with pure colours, noting that very little pigment is required, especially in deepening tones from light to dark. If the silk dries too quickly as you work, dampen it with a little more water.

It must be remembered that your colours will always be paler on a dampened surface. The water-alcohol mixture will help to preserve the whiteness of the silk and will also soften the colours. Always make sure you squeeze out your brush before putting it on to the silk.

You could experiment with this technique by using a *dry* brush on *dry* silk, applying pure colours. Further possible combinations include painting with watercolours on a wax or syrup impregnated fabric.

Summer set lip to earth's bosom bare,
And left the flushed print in a poppy there.

Francis Thompson

Designs

Michaelmas daisy

1) Square scarf, 'Haute couture'. Brocaded silk.
   Technique: paraffin wax, colours superimposed, see page 6.
2) Square scarf, 'Springtime'. Cotton veiling.
   Technique: template, crushed background, see page 8.
3) Long scarf, 'Lightness'. Crêpe georgette.
   Technique: direct painting on impregnated background, see page 8.
4) Sleeveless blouse, 'Nuances'. Brocaded silk.
   Technique: uncoloured gutta, see page 7.
5) Cushion, 'Gold and silver'. Brocaded silk.
   Technique: gold and silver gutta, see page 7.

Poppy

1) Square scarf, 'Misty'. Silk muslin.
   Technique: sugar-syrup, see page 10.
2) Long scarf, 'Proud poppies'. Pongé No 7.
   Technique: paraffin wax and tjanting, see page 6.
3) Pareo, 'Flame'. Lightweight cotton.
   Technique: positive and negative templates, see page 8.
4) Square scarf, 'Brilliance'. Crêpe de Chine.
   Technique: watercolour, see page 10.
5) Picture, 'Field of poppies'. Silk satin.
   Technique: watercolour, see page 10.
6) Picture, 'Sumptuous'. Silk satin.
   Technique: watercolour, see page 10.

Composition

1) Square shawl, 'Daisies, poppies and convolvulus'.
   Wool woven with gold thread.
   Technique: gold gutta and templates, see page 7.

Convolvulus

1) Square scarf, 'Classic'. Brocaded silk.
   Technique: uncoloured gutta, see page 7.
2) Long scarves, 'Black-and-white' and 'Navy blue'.
   Pongé No 9.
   Technique: false batik, see page 6.

3) Long scarf, 'Trellis'. Pongé No 9.
   Technique: false batik, see page 6.
4) Tablecloth, 'Pastoral'. Cotton.
   Technique: templates, see page 8.
5) Picture, 'Simplicity'. Silk satin.
   Technique: watercolour, see page 10.

Composition

1) Picture, 'Five flowers'. Crêpe de Chine.
   Technique: watercolour, with black accents, see page 10.

Rose

1) Square scarf, 'Memories'. Worsted wool.
   Technique: coloured gutta, see page 7.
2) Square scarf, 'Diaphanous'. Silk muslin.
   Technique: direct painting on impregnated background, see page 8.
3) Nightdress, 'Luxury'. Crêpe de Chine.
   Technique: template, see page 8.
4) Cushions, 'Yours and mine'. Brocaded silk.
   Technique: paraffin wax, see page 6.
5) Picture, 'Bouquet'. Pongé No 9.
   Technique: sugar-syrup and watercolour, see page 10.
6) Picture, 'Evening perfumes'. Silk satin.
   Technique: watercolour, see page 10.

Iris

1) Square scarf, 'Spangled'. Silk muslin.
   Technique: direct painting on impregnated background, plus sequins, see page 8.
2) Square scarf, 'Majestic'. Satin-striped crêpe.
   Technique: watercolour, see page 10.
3) Pareo, 'Irises'. Tinted silk.
   Technique: template, see page 8.
4) Square scarf, 'Shadows'. Silk twill.
   Technique: sugar-syrup, see page 10.
5) Picture, 'Magnificence'. Silk satin.
   Technique: watercolour, see page 10.

Michaelmas daisies

Of humblest friends, bright creature! Scorn not one:
The Daisy, by the shadow that it casts,
Protects the lingering dewdrop from the sun.

Wordsworth

Scarf, 'Haute couture'

Material: silk brocade, 120 × 120cm
(48 × 48in).

Technique: paraffin-wax base for
templates, overlaying wash of traditional colours.

Method: on damp silk, paint in
washes of yellow, blue and violet
with broad, sweeping strokes, leaving some areas white. Allow to dry
thoroughly.

Place your negative template on
the silk and apply the wax to the
spaces formed, ie, the flower shapes.
Allow to dry. Re-position the template as required and continue in this
way.

Finally, apply a black background
over the whole area and leave to dry.
Remove the wax. Fix the paints.

Scarf, 'Springtime'

Material: cotton veiling, 120 × 120cm (48 × 48in).

Technique: template placed on coloured and crushed background. Use thermofixable paints plus a thickening agent.

Method: cover all the fabric with paint, first yellow and then blue. Rub the cotton so that the colours are thoroughly powdered over the surface.

Press the material to smooth out the creases and let it dry. Add the thickening agent to some white paint. Place the negative template in position and fill in with white. Allow to dry. Position the second template for the stalk, leaves and centre and fill in with dark green.

Leave to dry thoroughly, then fix by ironing *both* sides of the fabric.

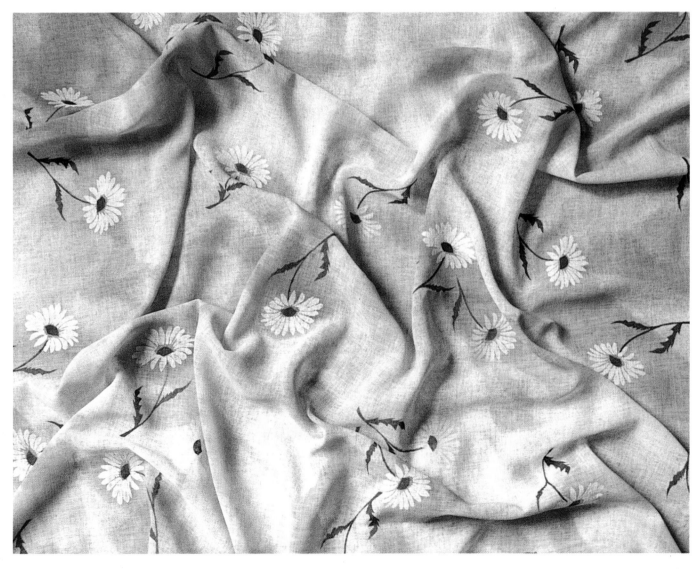

Long scarf, 'Lightness'

Material: crêpe georgette, 60 × 200cm (24 × 80in).

Technique: direct painting on an impregnated background with traditional colours.

Method: stretch the material and apply an anti-fusant mixture of one part gutta to six parts solvent with cotton wool. Leave to dry.

Place your drawing underneath the frame as it will clearly show through the transparent fabric. First paint in all the yellow petals, then the orange centres and, finally, the green stalks and leaves. Leave to dry.

Now add the brown and fix in the usual way.

Sleeveless blouse, 'Nuances'

Material: brocaded silk, 70 × 120cm (28 × 48in) for a child's version, 90 × 220cm (36 × 88in) for an adult.

Technique: traditional colours and untinted gutta.

Method: draw your design on tracing paper and place this under the stretched fabric. Apply the gutta lines.

Mix your colours for a rainbow effect and apply them in flat washes.

When the silk has been fixed, remove the gutta.

Cushion, 'Gold and silver'

Material: brocaded silk, 45 × 90cm (18 × 36in) for back and front. (45cm (18in) square).

Technique: gold and silver gutta and traditional colours.

Method: first apply the gold gutta and leave to dry, then the silver gutta. Allow to dry thoroughly.

Graduate the colours inside the gutta outlines, as well as around them. Normal fixing. Not to be dry-cleaned.

Poppies

But pleasures are like poppies spread –
You seize the flow'r, its bloom is shed;
Or like the snow falls in the river –
A moment white – then melts forever.

Robert Burns

Scarf, 'Misty'

Material: silk muslin, approximately 240 × 120cm (96 × 48in), noting that the silk is used double. (120 × 120cm (48 × 48in) square).

Technique: sugar-syrup and traditional colours.

Method: stretch the double thickness of silk on a frame. Roughly outline the poppies in sugar-syrup with a large brush, using a template if required. Check that both thicknesses have been penetrated by the syrup, if not, apply some on the reverse side.

'Blot' your paints over the background and flowers, then apply fresh areas of syrup over the colours and superimpose other colours. Leave to dry thoroughly.

Place the two thicknesses of silk, glued together by the syrup, in a purpose-built steamer and fix the paints by steaming. Protect the fabric on both sides with absorbent paper. After fixing, remove the sugar residue with lukewarm water.

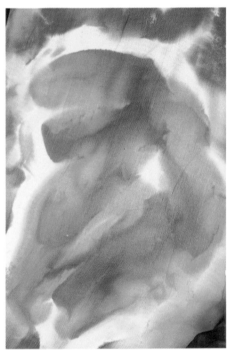

Long scarf, 'Proud poppies'

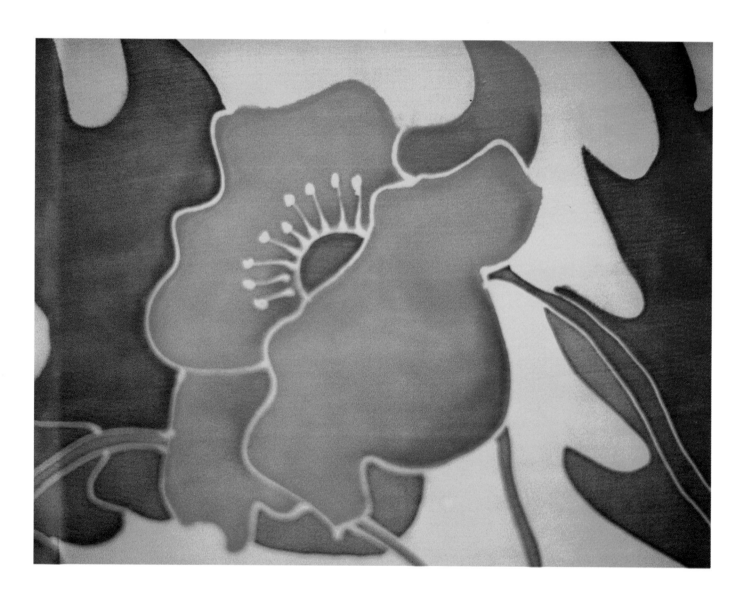

Material: pongé No 7, 45 × 150cm (18 × 60in).

Technique: paraffin-wax using a tjanting. Traditional colours.

Method: begin with a graduated background by preparing three different colours diluted with 50% water-alcohol mixture. Apply the first colour over one-third of the fabric working from the edge to the centre. If you are using a soft brush don't overload it. Now apply the second colour, overlapping the edge of the first, then the third. With a clean brush, rub the overlapping areas hard so that the colours really blend. Leave to dry.

Fill a tjanting with paraffin-wax, hold it at a slight angle and let the wax drip on to the silk without pressure.

Finally, begin colouring inside the areas of paraffin-wax. Colour spread over previously tinted silk will form a 'ring', so rub the material to blend the two 'pools' of colour.

Remove the wax before fixing the silk.

positive template

Pareo, 'Flame'

negative template

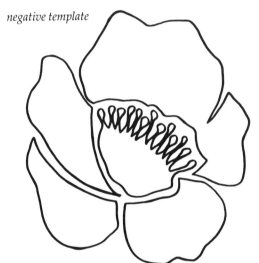

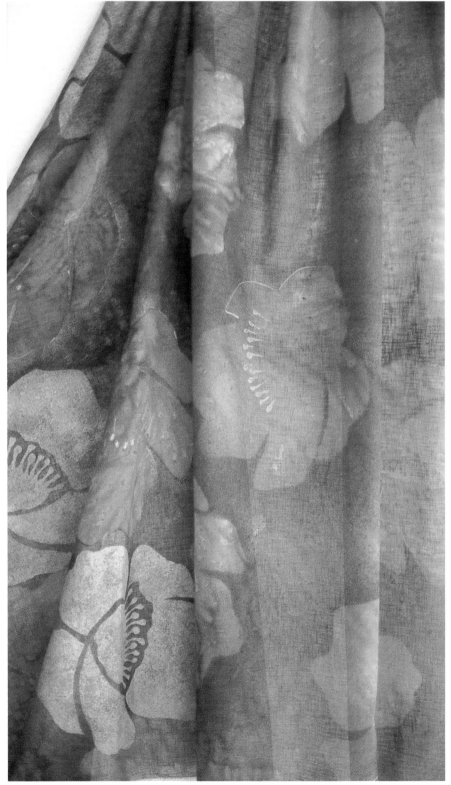

Material: thin cotton, 180 × 140cm (72 × 56in).

Technique: negative and positive templates, using thermofixable colours.

Method: work the background first. Stretch the cotton on a frame. Apply your 'flame' colours over the whole area and while still wet, sprinkle unrefined salt over some areas. When the cotton has dried, use a flat, hard brush to remove the salt.

Place your negative templates in position, trying to protect some of the salt effect, and keep these pressed on the fabric with small weights, such as pebbles. After painting, leave to dry then remove the templates. Take the fabric out of the frame to apply the positive templates. Using creamy gold paint, apply five gold poppies on the front of the pareo.

Allow to dry then fix with an iron.

detail of pareo motif

Scarf, 'Brilliance'

Material: crêpe de Chine, 90 × 90cm (36 × 36in).

Technique: watercolour using traditional colours.

Method: wet the silk and sponge away any surplus with household paper towels. Apply the light and medium tints, without saturating the brush, and leave some areas white.

Crush several colours in juxtaposition over the still wet background. This should be done quickly. When the paint is dry, add the accents with a dry brush and pure pigments. Finally, fix the paints.

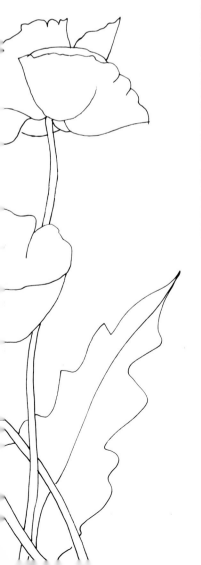

Picture, 'Field of poppies'

Material: white silk satin, 85 × 55cm (33 × 22in).

Technique: watercolour using traditional colours.

Method: on the dry silk, overlay the foreground poppies with paraffin-wax. Wet the silk with water, then paint in the background flowers. When these are dry, mask them with wax.

Now paint the background and leave to dry completely. Remove the wax surplus and fix the paints. Re-stretch the silk on the frame and wet the surface. When nearly dry, paint in the foreground blooms. When quite dry, add the details, such as stalks and leaves. Fix once more.

Picture, 'Sumptuous'

Material: white silk satin, 56 × 48cm (22 × 19in).

Technique: watercolour using traditional colours.

Method: work as given for the picture on page 26, masking the foreground flower.

Apply the background, leaving the area of the second poppy white. On almost dry silk, paint the flower and stalk in the background and the seed head in the foreground. Remove the wax and fix the paints.

Re-stretch the silk on the frame and work the foreground poppy with a *dry* brush on *dry* silk. Fix once more.

Composition

Shawl, 'Daisy, poppy and convolvulus'

Material: fine worsted wool with gold thread stripes, 120 × 120cm (48 × 48in).

Technique: gold gutta using traditional colours. Templates.

Method: as the fabric contains gold thread, outline your design with diluted gold gutta.

Prepare well-contrasted colours. Use a hard brush to colour in the templates. Rub the areas where the colours meet to blend them.

To finish, crush several tints all round the outer edges. Allow to dry thoroughly. Fix for longer than usual.

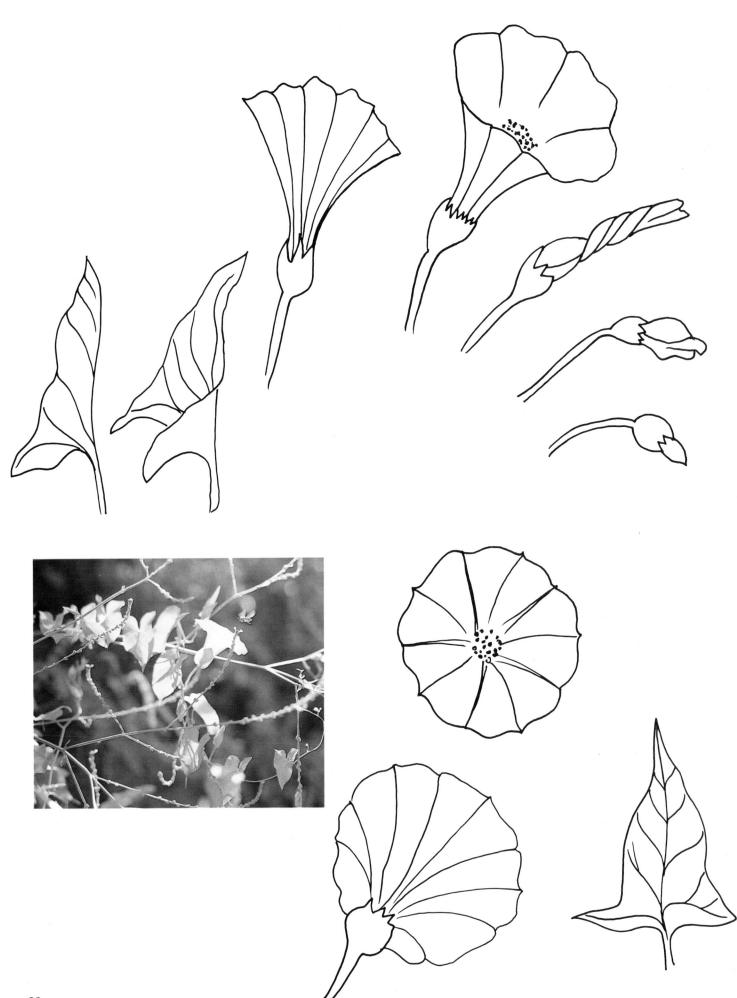

Convolvulus

Don't look at flowers with disdain,
look at their smile. How joyous it is!
Enough to make your head spin!

Chinese proverb.

All the convolvulus illustrations have one thing in common; the exploration of a chequered or striped background. This has been achieved partly through the texture of the fabric and partly with technique.

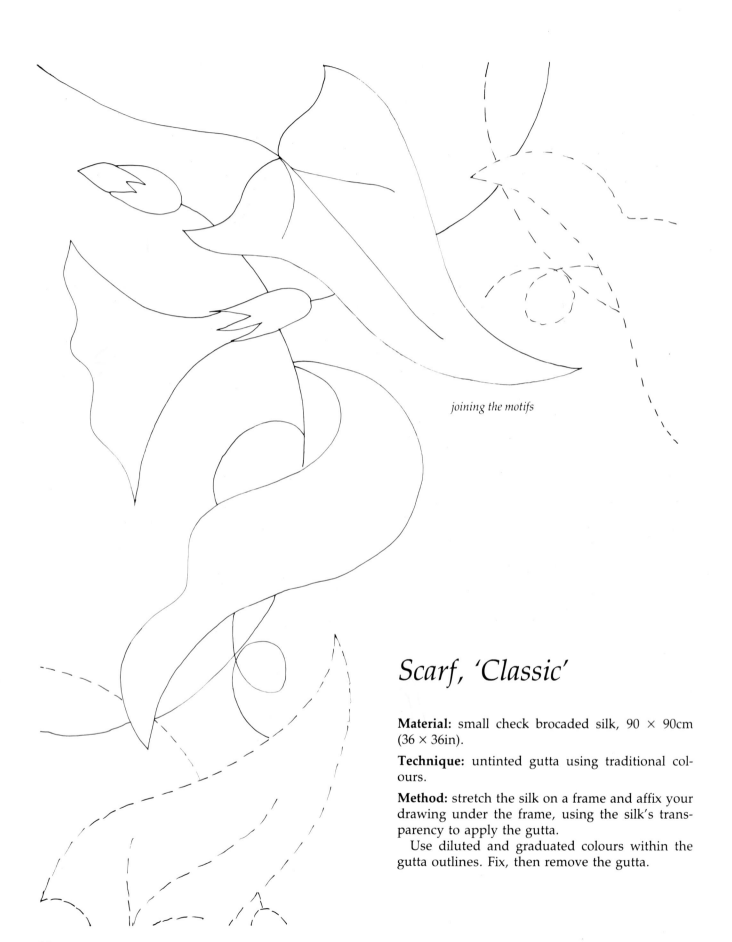

joining the motifs

Scarf, 'Classic'

Material: small check brocaded silk, 90 × 90cm (36 × 36in).

Technique: untinted gutta using traditional colours.

Method: stretch the silk on a frame and affix your drawing under the frame, using the silk's transparency to apply the gutta.

Use diluted and graduated colours within the gutta outlines. Fix, then remove the gutta.

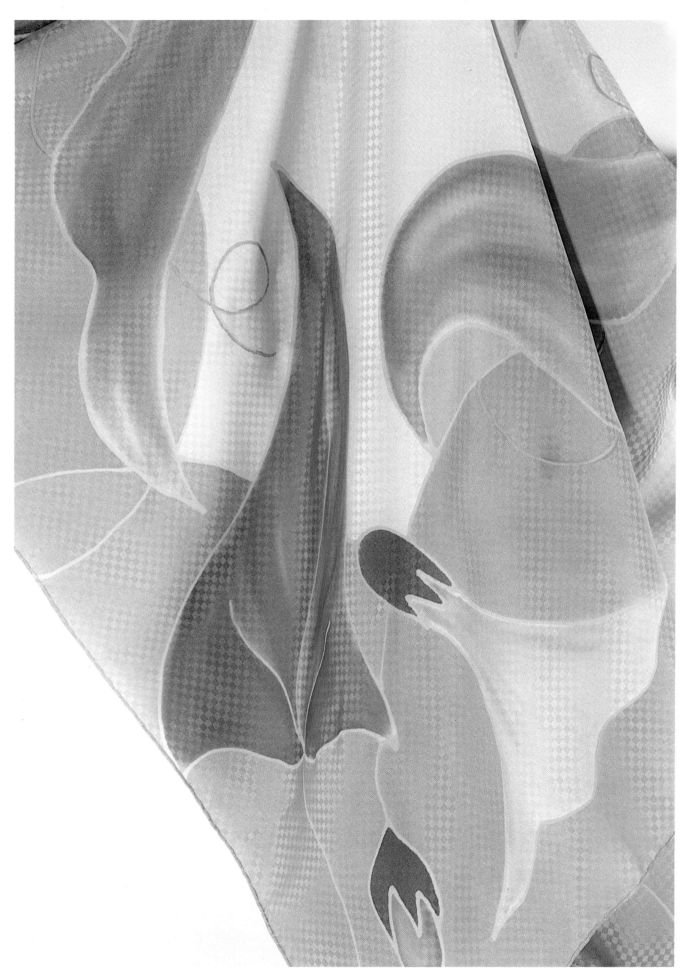

Long scarf, 'Black-and-white'

Material: pongé No 9, 45 × 150cm (18 × 60in).

Technique: false batik using traditional colours.

Method: make a charcoal drawing directly on the silk. Using a big, flat brush, spread paraffin-wax over the background area, making sure the wax does not come into contact with the charcoal lines.

Take the silk off the frame and rub it fairly hard to produce cracks in the wax. Re-stretch the silk on the frame. Paint a black background over the whole surface. The colour will penetrate the cracks as well as those areas free of wax. Carefully clean off any droplets of paint left on the wax with a damp cloth. Leave to dry.

Remove the wax, then fix.

Long scarf, 'Navy blue'

Material: white pongé No 9, 45 × 150cm (18 × 60in).

Technique: false batik using traditional colours.

Method: cover white silk with paraffin-wax, except for the white areas of your design. Apply a light blue background over the whole surface. Wipe off any droplets on the wax. Leave to dry.

On the light blue silk, cover the areas required in your design with paraffin-wax. Apply a mid-blue background over all and leave to dry. Remove the silk from the frame and rub it fairly hard to produce cracks in the wax but first fold the silk in a series of accordian pleats, first one way then the other.

Re-stretch the silk on the frame and paint the deep blue background over all.

Remove the wax, then fix.

For the motif design, see page 36.

motif for scarves on page 35

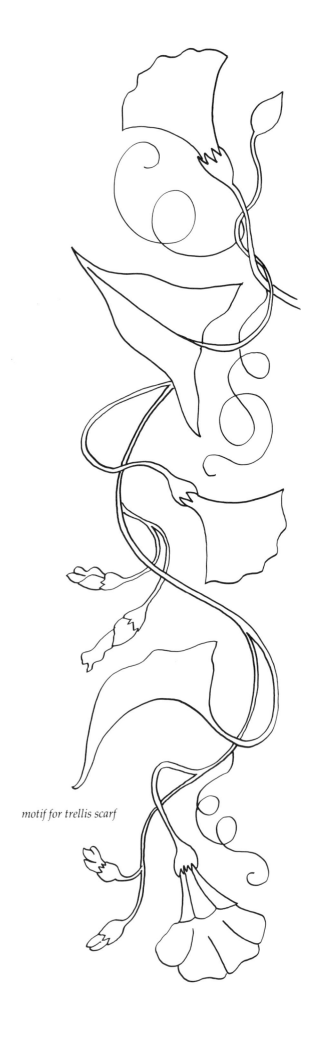

motif for trellis scarf

Long scarf, 'Trellis'

Material: pongé No 9, 45 × 150cm (18 × 60in).

Technique: false batik using traditional colours.

Method: on wet silk apply a pink hue on the areas of the flowers and buds. Dry, then protect these with paraffin-wax.

Apply a background of light blue over the surface. Allow to dry. Cover with paraffin-wax. Remove the silk from the frame and fold it in a series of lengthways pleats, then rub it hard to produce cracks in the wax.

Re-stretch the silk on the frame and paint a mid-blue background over all. Allow to dry. Now protect the veins, tendrils and central support and apply a dark blue background. Remove the wax, then fix.

Tablecloth, 'Pastoral'

Material: damask cotton, 160 × 160cm (64 × 64in).

Technique: templates, using thermofixable colours.

Method: place a piece of flannel over a table with a sheet of absorbent paper on top. Over this stretch the cotton, having previously ironed it well.

Trace your design with chalk and also draw a line for the border stripe.

Place your leaf template in position and using a stiff brush, blot in creamy thermofixable colour. When the whole motif has been applied, gently lift the template and repeat all round the fabric. Allow to dry.

Now position the flower template and work as given for the leaves. Use a dark colour to indicate the veins and stalks. Allow to dry before fixing with an iron.

Picture, 'Simplicity'

Material: white silk satin, 56 × 48cm (22 × 19in).

Technique: watercolour using traditional colours, and paraffin-wax.

Method: on the dry silk, cover the area of the motif with paraffin-wax. On wet silk, cover the background with pastel tints and leave to dry.

Place a piece of coarse netting with criss-cross pattern on top of the silk as flat as you can, then crush in several medium colours. Very gently lift the netting off and clean off with a damp cloth any colours left on the paraffin-wax. Remove the wax, fix and then wash.

Now apply the motif. Stretch the silk on a frame and wet the whole surface. Sketch in your flowers, leaves and stalks when the silk is almost dry. Once the silk is fully dry, complete the painting at leisure. Fix once more.

Composition of five flowers

Picture, 'Five flowers'

Material: crêpe de Chine, 40 × 50cm (16 × 20in).

Technique: watercolour using traditional colours.

Method: apply your light tones on stretched wet silk, leaving untouched the white areas in the background, the vase reflection and the lightened parts of the flowers.

Work from light to dark on damp silk first, and later on nearly dry silk. Having applied the colours, emphasize the outlines using an empty felt-tipped pen filled with dark colour, or an applicator with a small hole. Keep these outlines delicate, as illustrated.

Lydie Ottelart 89

Rose

What's in a name? That which we call a rose
By any other name would smell as sweet.

William Shakespeare

44

Scarf, 'Memories'

Material: worsted wool, 90 × 90cm (36 × 36in).

Technique: coloured gutta using traditional colours.

Method: prepare some yellow and black gutta, diluting with a little solvent. When spread over the wool, the gutta should be fluid enough to seep into the material. If it doesn't completely penetrate the fibres, re-do the whole design on the back of the fabric. Use paper cones rather than a metal applicator, which will be impeded by the loose threads of the wool, and apply the gutta with an even pressure.

Leave to dry thoroughly before painting inside the outlines. Fix for longer than normal.

Material: silk muslin, 140 × 140cm (56 × 56in).

Technique: direct painting over an impregnated surface using traditional colours.

Method: stretch the silk on a frame and apply a graduated pink background. To achieve tonal graduation, prepare a pure colour with a mixture of 50% water and alcohol. Divide this into three containers, keeping one of the original mixture, then adding more dilutant to each of the remaining two, to obtain middle and light tones.

Begin by applying the darkest tone with a soft brush which is not over-loaded, starting from the outer edge. Next apply the medium tint, overlapping the first, and end with the palest shade, overlapping as before. Rub these overlapping areas with a clean brush to ensure that they blend well. Leave to dry.

Apply an anti-fusant of one part gutta to six parts solvent over the whole surface, without saturating it. Allow to dry thoroughly.

Hold your drawing under the frame and paint directly on to the silk. Take care to let one colour dry thoroughly before placing another next to it, or covering it with another. Fix in the normal way.

Nightdress, 'Luxury'

Material: crêpe de Chine, 90 × 200cm (36 × 80in). Lace trimming, optional.

Technique: template design, using traditional and iridescent thermofixable colours.

Method: to apply the design, insert absorbent paper between the front and back of the nightdress. Fix your template with adhesive tape to the front of the gown and blot in the different colours, graduating the tones in both the flowers and leaves. Fix with an iron.

To colour the background, cover a table with cloth, then absorbent paper on top of it. Place the silk on top of this and gently rub it, then crush in several colours, alternating them over the area. Allow to dry, then fix.

48

Cushions, 'Yours and mine'

Material: silk damask, 45 × 90cm (18 × 36in), for back and front (45cm (18in) square).

Technique: paraffin-wax using traditional colours.

Method: the silk is already patterned with tiny roses and the stylized motif represents the heart of a rose. Both cushions have the same background, which consists of coloured blots of paint, splashed with water. Leave to dry.

Left-hand cushion: fill in the outline of the motif and the border edges with paraffin-wax, on the front only. Apply a dark colour over the unwaxed areas.

Right-hand cushion: apply paraffin-wax for the outlines of the motif, on the front only. Apply a dark colour over the whole area.

Picture, 'Bouquet'

Material: pongé silk No 9, 52 × 48cm (21 × 19in).

Technique: sugar-syrup and watercolour, using traditional colours.

Method: work background and subject simultaneously with pale tints on a wet surface. Allow to dry. Cover the vase with paraffin-wax. With a fine brush, apply sugar-syrup to the roses, leaving interstices.

Wet the silk once more, keeping water away from the sugar-syrup areas. On the background and blossoms, apply the middle tints then the deeper tones.

Allow the silk to dry. Using the watercolour method, apply the stalks and leaves. Remove the wax. Fix and then wash.

Picture, 'Evening perfumes'

Material: silk satin, 42 × 55cm (17 × 22in).

Technique: paraffin-wax and watercolour, using traditional colours.

Method: cover the motif with paraffin-wax. Wet the silk all round this area then paint the background. Leave to dry. Remove the wax, fix and wash.

Stretch the silk on a frame. On dry silk, paint the flowers and leaves with a brush lightly dipped in pure colours. In order to soften what can sometimes be a harsh effect with this method, use a fine brush to apply 95° proof alcohol over the separate paint areas. Dry rapidly with a hair dryer. Fix the paints again.

Iris

To see a world in a grain of sand,
And a heaven in a wild flower,
Hold infinity in the palm of your hand,
And eternity in an hour.

William Blake

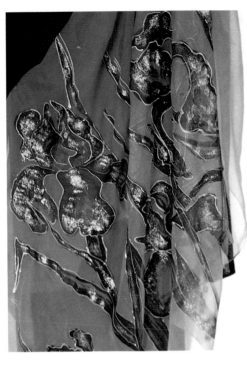

Scarf, 'Spangled'

Material: coloured silk muslin, 140 × 140cm (56 × 56in). Small sequins or glass beads.

Technique: direct painting on to impregnated background, using liquid thermofixable colours.

Method: stretch the coloured silk on to a frame and apply anti-fusant evenly over the whole area. Leave to dry.

Paint the motifs directly on to the silk with coloured washes, ie, spreading a single colour with water. Allow to dry.

Apply a fabric adhesive very sparingly over required areas and sprinkle with very tiny gold, silver and purple sequins, or beads. When dry, strengthen the outlines with dry white paint.

Remove from the frame, shake to remove surplus sequins, then fix.

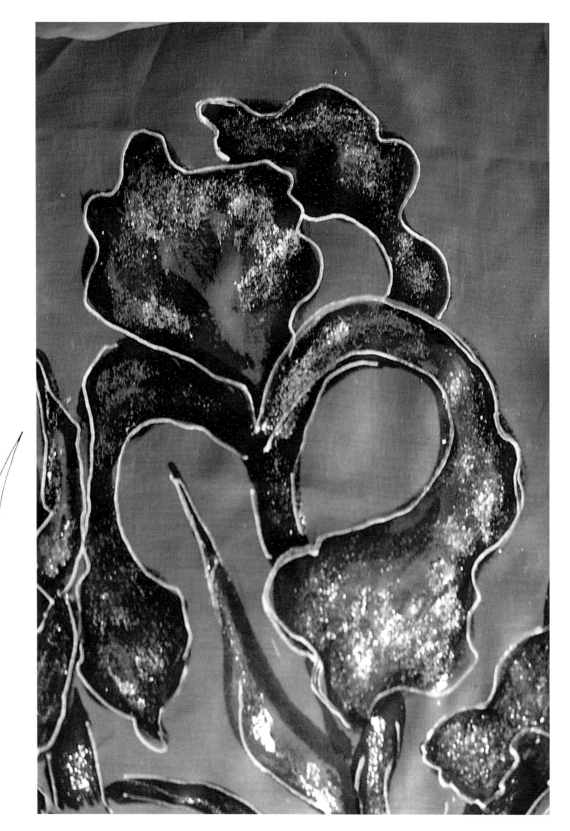

Scarf, 'Majestic'

Material: satin striped, silk crêpe, 90 × 90cm (36 × 36in).

Technique: watercolour, using traditional colours.

Method: stretch the silk on a frame and cover entirely with water. When still damp, apply all the light and middle tints with an unsaturated brush.

Crush in several colours alternately over the background, as if you were beating a drum. When the silk is dry, complete the motifs with pure colour. Allow to dry, then fix.

Pareo, 'Irises'

Material: coloured silk, 140 × 250cm (56 × 100in).

Technique: template, using thermofixable colours.

Method: along the lower edge of the fabric, mark the positions for each repeat of the motif to achieve a continuous frieze.

Place a large sheet of absorbent paper on a suitable flat surface and cover with a piece of colourfast, slightly damp material. Place the lower edge of the silk on top of this. Using a negative template and white paint, colour in the motif. Gently remove the template and allow the paint to dry, then reposition for the next motif. Allow to dry and when complete, fix with an iron.

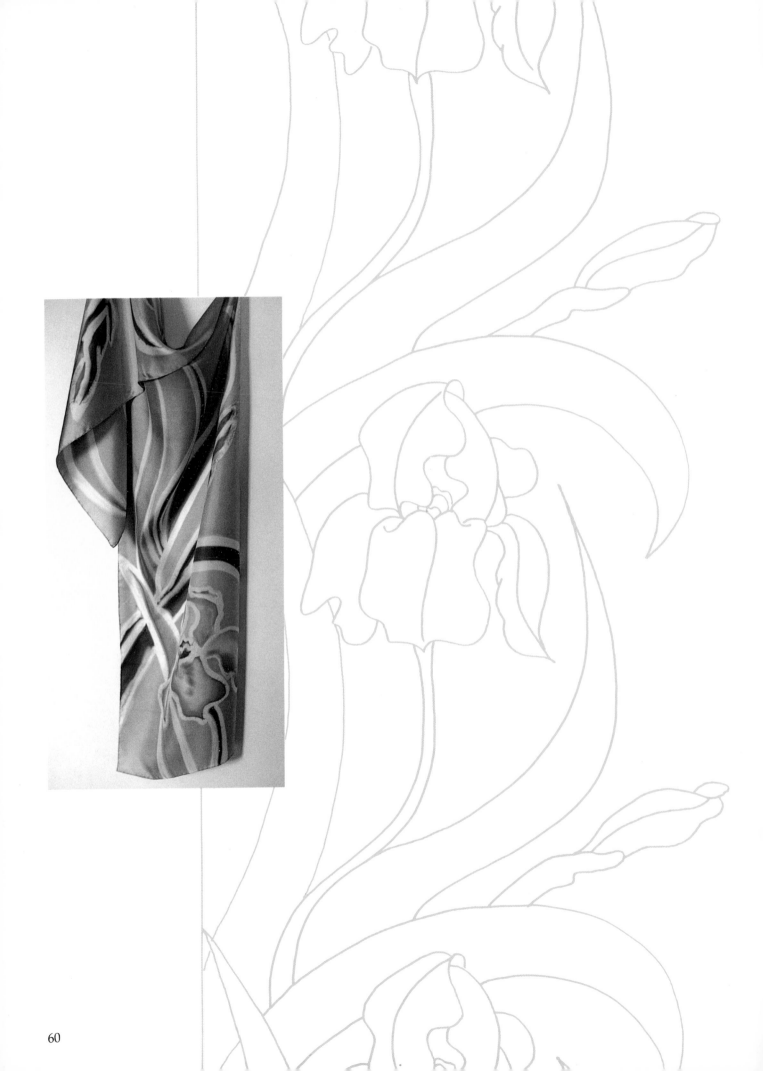

Long scarf, 'Shadows'

Material: silk twill, 45 × 150cm (18 × 60in).

Technique: sugar-syrup, using traditional colours.

Method: stretch the silk on a frame and draw in the outlines of your motif with charcoal.

Prepare a thick sugar-syrup and apply this with a pointed brush over the charcoal outlines, in a continuous line. Place the paints inside the syrup outlines and apply the background round them. Leave to dry overnight. Fix and wash.

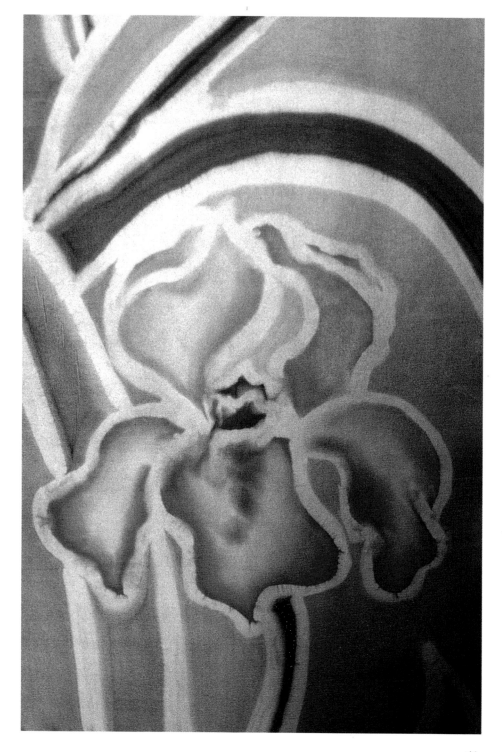

Picture, 'Magnificence'

Material: white silk satin, 56 × 86cm (22 × 34in).

Technique: watercolour using traditional colours.

Method: on the white background, cover the foreground flowers and leaves with paraffin-wax. Cover one flower and bud in the middle distance with wax.

Place the silk in a frame and cover the background with water. When still damp, paint the flowers in the background and all the remaining leaves. Allow to dry. Remove the wax and fix.

Stretch the silk on the frame again. Using a pointed brush dipped in pure colour, paint the areas previously covered on to the dry silk. Fix again.